Preface

I thank my family for all their support and guidance during this journey

I also thank my friends and God for all the light, faith and love

Introduction

If you found your way to this book, it may be you are looking for ways to create more wealth for yourself, your family and others.

A book can also be a conversation between friends, so I thank you for your time, time being our most precious resource, since we cannot buy or create more as with wealth.

We live in complex times, where value and money dictate freedom and power. Globalisation and technology have made everything easier to access but a lot more competitive at the same time, reason why it is important to create value for others in order to survive, thrive and evolve.

In this book we will start by analysing how to manage your money and income, your needs and spendings. Then we will move into value and wealth creation, followed by safe investment strategies.

Thank you for choosing this book, I hope it helps you make great investments, and leads you to a healthy, happy and prosperous life.

Godspeed!

Miguel Oliveira

Master in Advanced Architecture by IaaC

founder of bricoarts.com

Managing Money

It seems everything is getting more expensive.

I'm sure you've heard this and may even have said it some times. Indeed, every year some things get more expensive than others. While inflation may vary from year to year, houses, cars, clothes, food and many other products and services tend to increase its cost over time.

House

Let's talk about your house. When you are young and your worklife is still unstable, renting can be a good option. Tipically, houses in the center have more expensive rents than houses in the suburbs, but transportation costs and times must also be taken into account. So if you are renting, consider all your expenses in daily commuting to see whether you are saving time and money living where you are.

When you get a more stable work and social life, it might be a better option to buy a house rather than rent one. Here's where it gets especially tricky for most people. A house is probably the greatest investment most people will ever make in their lifetime, and still most people buy overbudgeted, oversized houses they don't need.

Let me repeat this: overbudgeted and oversized.

When buying a house, make sure you buy something that won't put a heavy load in your finances. If you opt for a credit, and finance your house with a bank, make sure you make a downpayment as high as possible thus reducing your credit as much as possible, because interest rates, even when sold cheap, over time will eat away most of your wealth. Some managers advise a maximum of a 30% credit limit (including house, car and credit card) from all your montly income, however the lower, the better.

So its better to save money for a downpayment, and buy a house that answers your real needs. Again, regarding location, you must value your time and transportation costs to see what is better for you, city center or suburbs.

Most people opt for new, ready to live houses or apartments. While this may save trouble and stress, it is rarely a good deal. It's sort of like buying the newest smartphone out of the store as soon as its launched, for a premium price of course. If you want to get a good deal in your house, consider buying an old house or apartment, or a piece of land, and building it yourself.

Yes it´s stressful, reason why it saves a lot of money. But its better to suffer some stress for 1 or 2 years during construction, or reconstruction of a house, than 40 years of stress paying an overpriced house and mortgage, that reduces your wealth creation and finantial freedom.

Look for what others don´t value, but be very careful analysing the ammount of money you will need for the repairs and construction. Find an experient and honest architect and construction manager, to help you estimate your building costs and schedules, before you buy any house. The best construction managers can even help you quantify the market value of any house or site, and they will help you get a good deal so you don´t buy an overpriced piece of realestate.

You can run some numbers online, doing averages of prices per square meter or foot, to figure out the average costs in the locations you are interested in. This can help you filter out some houses, but only an honest and experienced architect and construction manager can help you assess the real value in both the house and in the construction works needed.

Go for a safe, not too big or too high house, with adequate, resistant and lasting materials you can afford. Think you can improve it over time, so first make it functional and confortable. Again, a good experienced architect and construction manager will help you in the whole process. Hire construction workers independently, buy all the materials yourself and do as much construction work as you safely can. Use renewable energy and efficient materials, infrastructures and appliances thay save you money and save the planet as well.

In the end, you will be amazed of how much money you saved, and how much value you created out of your courage, energy and work.

Car

A car would be the second greatest investment for most people in their lives, when adding up fuel costs, insurance, repairs and taxes, provided you really need one. Some people live in the center, and can pretty much do their entire life without a car. They rent a car if they need one. However, due to the freedom a car provides, most people will eventually buy a car at some point in their lives.

Again, like a house, buy a car you can afford to own and maintain, especially a reliable one. Japanese tend to make reliable cars, proven safe electric cars that have few moving parts can also be a good choice. The best car you can buy isn't brand new, it ranges from an one year old demonstration or service car to a four to five years long end of lease car from companies or individuals.

A car under 5 years of age and under 100.000kms or 60.000 miles, if proven reliable by most users, is a great buy for you will be able to buy it at a significant discount, compared to a new car. Usually under these criteria, you can get a discount in the 40% to 50% range, even higher in some cases. Always have a professional independent honest mechanic check its computer logs, mechanic parts and ride you before you buy it, to make sure you're buying a good product.

Again, avoid buying a credit for your car, pay as much in cash as you can. Also remember to maintain it properly, following recommended service intervals and using reliable parts and components. In most cases OEM original certified parts are the wiser and safer choice, especially regarding most of the complex essential mechanic and electronic systems in your car, that will keep it running for a long long time, at least 400.000kms or 250.000 miles.

To assess when its time to change car, do the following math: when yearly repair costs, without including regular maintenance rise above let´s say, 1.500€ in europe or 2.000$ in the US, mainly because labour costs are higher in the US, maybe its time to get another car. But this would have to happen almost every year, or 2 to 3 years in a row. So really most people don´t need to change their cars, they choose to.

It´s not a need, its a want...

Clothes and Food

By now you are beginning to gain a deep focus on what has real and stable value to us humans: essentials. In good times or bad times, we always need essentials. Clothes and food are among those needs.

I´m no expert in fashion, textiles or shoes industries. I know some family members, friends and clients that are, however I´m not sure they make good choices regarding their foods and clothes. This is a very specific and personal area, so disregard what I'm about to say if it doesn't help you, you'll understand why in a while.

From my experience with most premium brands, with the exception being very few, I have found premium products to be of poor quality in the long run. It seems they are made for people who use them for a while and then get rid of them. So, I couldn't see the value in those products and I began to buy regular brands, that would last as much, and in some cases even more than premium brands. I pay special care to components, zips, buttons, textile resistance, to evaluate the quality of the product, and I will only buy what I need in sales or promotions.

Here's why this might not help you or make sense to you. I know perfectly bright and focused humans that add value to society, that buy premium fashionable brands and feel good about it. It gives them a sense of belonging and joy. If a product can do that, it has value. So if buying some premium clothes and shoes once in a while makes you feel better, more confident and do better work and investments, that might make sense. You really have to dig into the reason why you like a certain product or brand, and make sure you get as much value of it as possible, without disregarding its quality, otherwise its just pure value speculation and throwing away your hard earned money...

Regarding food, we all need to eat and drink, and should value quality instead of quantity. A healthy diet will give you a pretty healthy body and mind, thus allowing you to work and invest better, while spending less in healthcare support.

In terms of nights out and meals in restaurants and bars, one should be very careful not to burn a lot of money in those leisure activities. Once in a while its great, but don't fall in the trap of making it a habit, one you'll become addicted to.

Other Products and Services

In regard to other products and services, as tech, gadgets, tools, education (I think of it as a tool) think of it this way: if they help you do better work, create better products and services, and make better investments, they make sense. But don't fool yourself buying the top smartphone, laptop and tablet, when the lower end models can provide you with all the tools you need, usually at 50% cost and weight too!

Regarding education, this is a tricky subject, again very personal. As the tool it is, its good to have one than have none. Whether the top university and faculty add that much value to your future worklife, that's something only you can sense and feel. Visit the schools you are interested in before choosing one, and get a feel for the spaces and people there. Analyse the work they produce and see if it has value, even if you don't understand it. Some times getting a glimpse into the future or a new way to approach problems comes with a premium price, and its worth it. Some other times its just speculation and useless fog.

Run some numbers, regarding what value those tools will add to you, and get other specialists opinions to find the best ones for you, those that will allow you to do the best work of your life.

Summary

This chapter's point was to give you an important insight into managing your expenses and money well.

There is a saying "who isn't able to manage 1000$ isn't able to manage 1.000.000$" and this is the reason why a lot of fast made wealth fades away.

Think of this chapter as the foundations of your investment personality, and remember...

...something you don't need is always too expensive.

Adding Value

So, what is value and how do we create it?

Value can be defined as an inherent capacity that a person, product, material or service can have, that is greater than the sum of its parts. Art can have great value, a value greater than the cost of the canvas and paints used to create it, in the case of a great painting. Art creates emotions and experiences in us, that make us feel good and special. That is priceless and if your product or service triggers an emotional positive response, you'll be on your way to great value creation.

The more people you provide value to, while helping them feel good and solving their problems, the more value and wealth you will create.

So, focus on people, find out their problems and needs. You'll be surprised with what people look for, especially on the internet. Most times you will find products and services keywords that you had no idea of, simply because they don't make that much sense to you, or you just don't need them or value them like most people do.

Remember to find a balance between what you like/need and what people like/need, if you want to create great value and wealth. The more you focus just on what you like, the more you'll get into a smaller niche, that eventually can be so small there's only you in it... If you focus only on what people like, you may not like your work and lose inspiration and motivation, especially if you're a creative person. Be careful about this analysis and find the right balance.

Products and Services

One way of creating value and wealth is to sell products and services that people need. The other way is by investing. In this chapter we will focus on creating products and services.

Most services usually have a problem, unless you have a lot of workers or franchised networks, that is you only make money when you are physically working, as is the case of a lawyer, a doctor, an architect and an engineer. Products, on the other hand, can generate value and wealth even when you are sleeping.

Services, especially as a freelancer, have little associated costs. Products have great associeted costs, for patents, tools, machines, buildings, workers, permits... Building and managing a factory is an epic energy consuming task. If that is your passion and what you are good at, godspeed and good luck.

If you choose to be in the, apparently, safer path of services, make sure you are an expert in your field and solve the hardest problems people may have. Build a strong network of professionals that you can trust and collaborate independently with. Keep updating your skills and knowledge, and make sure its work you love, so it won't feel like work; that will make it all easier and better.

You can create products and/or services online too, with little costs. Finding and connecting your audience will be tremendously hard, especially if you don't use paid advertising, which can eat away your wealth. There are two ways to promote a product or service, by working yourself a lot and spreading the word and contents online and physically, or by paying someone else to do it for you.

Most of the companies and brands you know use credit and advertising as leverage to sustain their businesses. That is very very risky, especially during hard times, and requires a very high competitive advantage to stay afloat. Again, avoid credit as much as you can, and only use it if the return, that the tools you bought with that credit provide, is exponential and certain.

A true digital marketing expert can give you great results, but make sure they offer data for return on investment that is realistic. Don't spend 1000$ in ads to sell 100$ worth of products and services, even if they say you're investing in building brand awareness...

Instead, or simultaneously, create great products and services that people need and like, and customers will spread the word online and physically for you. Real value, when shown to the right people, sooner or later creates great wealth. Stay focused, and keep working and going.

Now, when I talk about creating products and services, I don't mean for you to quit your job tomorrow and start working only on your own business right away. Many people strike a good balance working for someone and building their company and business in their spare time. This is a safer approach, however there may be some risks in this approach too.

Sometimes, the only way to create a great product or service, is to walk alone the hard road of obstacles it requires. Mainly, because one needs to feel the urge to succeed, as if there is no other option. Being 100% on that path can produce better results than working for someone else and putting only 10% of your time, focus and energy in your company and business. So be careful about your commitment, focus and safety nets.

Again, this is a very personal decision, know yourself, test yourself. Many times others won't have a clue of what is best for you, and they will advise only what they would do in that same situation. However, listen to all of them politely and humbly, sometimes they will provide valuable insight in the middle of all the critiques. And don't poke the lions in their eyes...

Always seek honest and true opinions and advice from others, even if it hurts to hear them, but don't allow yourself to be brought down by their frustration and negativity. Always rise above the occasion and see growth opportunity in chaos and crisis.

Investing

Another way of creating value and wealth is by investing. Think of investing as seeds that you may create, plant, look after, grow and harvest.

In a way, creating your own business where you sell products and/or services can also be investing. Buying tools and education, can also be investing. And connecting with the right people, can also be investing.

About people, look for positive people in all your connections. Of course all of us are entitled to have some bad days and bad cycles, but that doesn't entitle people to abuse or mistreat others. Be very mindful about this when you connect with anyone on any level. In some cases 1+1 equals 2, in some cases 1+1 equals 11, but in some cases 1+1 equals 0 and might even equal -2... Again, this is very personal, and will depend on your character and resistance to negativity, something only you can evaluate by the way you feel when its present.

Somehow positivity manages to create better results. But not blinded positivity, more like faith that things will always work out, for we need to rationally and intuitivelly assess data as it is, not just by wishful thinking which is a way to disaster.

Back to investing as seeds. You can invest your work, your time and your money. The idea is that for every unit you invest, in time you will get a return of several units, multiplying your initial investment.

There are basically two kinds of investment strategies. One is growth and value investing, which is sustained by real value, and although it may fall in price during bad times, in the end it always recovers. The other is speculative investing, where prices go up but the value isn't there and never will be.

This one is very very complicated, and appears from cycle to cycle. The 2000's dotcom crisis and the 2008 subprime crisis were both caused by speculative investing, where people where buying into overvalued investments that didn't have the value or security that justified the price they were selling for. While speculative investing can seem logical when everyone else is doing it and the rewards may be huge, and in some cases some people reap them, its like putting all your hard earned money in a casino. Usually a lot of people always lose their money, and everyone directly or indirectly, ends up paying the heavy price of the finantial crisis through taxes and governments bailouts...

So, when investing look for real growth value, that might be underpriced, or if priced correctly, will grow in time. You can assess real value through data available on the internet, averaging prices, comparing investments, costs, fees, taxes and returns. Do remember to factor in all taxes and expenses related to your investments, for they cut away a part of your return, and be very mindful about this part.

Look for independent professional honest advisors for guidance in different places, your bank, your accountants, your lawyers, your realestate agents, your fellow workers, and gather as much data as you can. Avoid investing in fashionable trends, without doing your numbers on its real value and projected growth overtime, always considering the worst case scenario.

Realestate

Realestate is one of the essentials we need to live. That makes it an excellent investment, as long as its bought and built at the right value.

As in every investment, there can also be speculation in the realestate market. So you need to assess the real value for what that piece of realestate should be selling for, compared to the price people are asking for it. Sometimes its better to wait or simply walk away from a deal. If you buy overpriced, and I have once in my first deals, it gets very difficult to add value to the building and profit from the investment, especially when factoring in taxes and construction costs.

So do the averages and price comparing online, and talk to your trusted realestate agents, architects, contruction managers and builders, to get the real value on the buildings or land you may want to invest in.

You can approach realestate investing in two major ways, (I don´t know REITs enough and don´t really value them a lot since I wouldn't own the whole real building):

1. renting it for an annual return on your invested capital;

2. selling it for a profit to someone else (that may be investors or families).

Always buy cheap undervalued realestate, and spend as little as you can in construction, doing all the works you safely can and buying all the materials as well. Then you may choose to rent it for a while and sell it once an economic cycle is good to sell.

In realestate demand and centricity play a very important role in price and value. Its better to invest in a bad building in a good location than investing in a good building in a bad location.

In case you invest to rent, we'll suppose you buy an old house for 25.000€, and spend 25.000€ in the repairs and construction. Your total investment should be around 50.000€. If you rent it for 500€ every month, you should have an approximate return of 10% every year for your invested capital. A 5% to 10% return these days is good, but you should aim for 10% as rule of thumb, that will keep you from getting into a bad deal when doing numbers before you invest.

In case you invest to sell, also known as house flipping, lets use the same case, you bought it for 25.000€ and spent 25.000€ in construction, having invested a total of 50.000€. You should at least sell it for a 50% clean profit, after all taxes and selling expenses have been paid. That means you will probably have to sell it for at least 90.000€. Here is where it gets tough. Remember value in a painting being more than just the sum of its canvas and paints? Its the same with realestate. You can invest little money and add great value, but for that you will need to ensure a safe, functional, comfortable, sustainable and aesthetically pleasing building. And here is where most realestate investors fail.

Most people think they know enough, and choose to do everything themselves without seeking professional technical advice. Only a good experient architect and construction manager can help you add the value you seek, in order to make a good profit and a good investment.

Look for one that invests in realestate himself as well. Its a very different game investing his money or investing someone else's money. An architect that has invested his money, and has gone through the painful experience of buying, rebuilding and selling, will be better prepared to help you make good choices when the time comes.

Good and trustworthy builders, construction materials stores, realestate agents, lawyers, accountants will also be an essential part of your dream team. As they say, you can always be right and know everything or you can be successful. You can't always have both.

Now, let's specifically talk about realestate location. It is important to choose a place with activity, lots of people, business and nearby public facilities and transports. Where there are people and businesses, there is value and money.

I advise you to study a map of the city or area where you want to invest, like a satellite view, and add pins or circles to the most important business centers and public facilities in that area, such as universities, hospitals and public services. You should be looking for buildings and activities that will remain there for a long time, and that add value to their communities and surroundings.

After you identified some areas, ideally neighbourhood size in radius, or streets, it is time to hit the road.

First, drive around your selected areas and study parking spaces and access to highways and other infrastructures. Then park your car, and walk around talking to people such as neighbours and workers. Walking and talking is the best way to sense a place and get real feedback.

Trust your gut, if you sense something isn't right, try to identify what it is, and after you have rationalized it, make a decision. Some places are apparently perfect, others awful, but the underlying truth and energy of a place goes way beyond appearances.

Sometimes a place or a building can look a mess but be a real rough diamond, with nice and friendly neighbours. This was the case in my recent investment in a neighbourhood's old house from 1930. The house was in ruins and some people advised me not to buy it, but the more I talked to neighbours and sensed the site, the more I felt it was a great investment. It is located in a quiet place behind the local shopping center, nearby hospital and street market, in the entrance of the city center. Tenants can do their entire life without needing a car if they choose to, that's value.

Despite the ruins look to this house and others in the neighbourhood, it had potential, and other investors are now doing the same, refurbishing nearby houses. So walk & talk and you'll find great opportunities.

Your trustworthy realestate agents will also help you find great opportunities, and the internet is also a great place to look. However there is nothing like going there yourself and analysing the location and the condition of the building.

Keep a spreadsheet with all your data, costs, averages, expenses, taxes and predictions. This way you will be able to know if an investment is sound.

Stocks and ETFs

By now we've covered value and wealth creation in products, services and realestate.

Many successful investors praise the stockmarket, securities and commodities as excellent investments as well. I have been studying the stock market for some years, and I do believe there can be ocasional good opportunities for investment there as well.

The trick is again related to price, value and valuation. If you buy stocks, bonds or commodities you will want to buy them undervalued and/or great growth potential.

It's really quite simple. The difficulty comes in assessing the real value and growth accurately. That can be done analysing a company or investment, its debt ratios, its liquidity and money available, its assets, inventories, past growth and future growth and its competitive advantage and situation in the market.

Many websites and platforms provide this data for free or in paid subscriptions. Again, if you want to save and do most of the work yourself, while gaining a better insight at a company and investment, I recommend your search and read the free 10K annual reports and Q4 quartely reports of that company. Look for tables and numbers, there's usually a lot of text more or less subjective, but numbers have to be objective and are regulated by securities commitees.

Many great investors recommend buying what you know, and this is also simple and complex at the same time. When they say buy what you know, it means buying some part of a business that you can understand and continuously value. A part of a business because stocks are parts of that underlying company and business. When you own stocks of a company, you actually own a fraction of that company, and in some cases if the company pays dividends to its shareholders, or stock owners, you'll get paid a small part of their profits from time to time.

So far I have only invested time and money in the US stock market, mainly due to its liquidity, size, regulating agencies, and the dynamic entrepreneur character of the US economy. I am able to find great value in the NYSE and the NASDAQ markets, and I avoid other markets that I don't know as well, which doesn't mean you should too.

Again, invest in something you know, and always be prepared for the worst.

My advisors told me to invest a maximum of 5% of my money in the stock market, as a defensive approach. Some people stretch this limit to 10%. Others stretch even more, but the risk increases considerably then, and in case of a crash or a downturn correction in the price of your stocks, you can lose money or have to hold those stocks for a long number of years until they recover.

This is why great investors advise investing long term. If you buy stocks of a great company, at fair value or even better, undervalued regarding its market value or even its book value, and the company has a great competitive advantage and is expected to keep growing over time, you have made a great investment. Even in the case of a crash or big downturn, usually every ten years these days for some strange reason, when the stock drops in market price more than 40%, over time it will recover its value, usually in 2 to 5 years time. However that will depend a lot on the economy, unemployment, inflation and interests rates.

Some investors like to invest in ETFs and index funds instead of single stocks. Think of ETFs and index funds as buckets of many stocks, bonds and other finantial instruments. Since they have a lot of elements, even if one fails, the others compensate.

It is a safer approach that reaps great profits in the long term. Many people preach S&P500 ETFs and tracking funds, but be careful to analyse the fund management costs, for they can eat a lot of your profits over time. Also make sure the ETF's or funds managing companies are sound and safe finantially. An ETF like the S&P500 growing at an average of 10% every year will compound overtime in a curve like exponential growth, which is pretty awesome. Do some math online in compounding interests and investment calculators, you'll be amazed with the possible returns. But always remember to subtract inflation, usually around 2% realistically, and taxes.

That realistic 2% yearly inflation, if you factor in your house and utilities as well as other living costs, also means that every year the money you have standing still in the bank devaluates 2% from its value set at time you made it. In 10 years time it will have lost value around 20% and in 20 years time you will have lost in value almost half of what you made in the beggining.

So this is a case when standing still is actually more risky than investing, so try to invest at least 2% of your earnings every year. This is very, very important!

Regarding where and how to buy these investments, I recommend you use the safest possible traders. I use my bank, which is state owned. Sure I pay higher commissions than in web platforms or other banks, but my banks' support, finantial security and insurances give me the safety I value, especially because I am a long term value and growth investor.

This doesn't mean you can't trade securities and commodities in some safe trading web platforms, but always read the contracts thorougly, you may find the risk you are taking in the case of a crash or economic downturn is too high. Again, find out what kind of investor you are and what kind of risks you are willing to take.

So, in conclusion, buy what you know and can valuate, and understand the dynamics that can affect its growth. Be prepared for great downturns and crashes along the way, and hold on to your great investments if they are sound, regardless of what the market is offering for them, at least until you think its time to collect your profit and earnings.

Avoid speculative fashionable trendy investments, for they behave more like a casino, and remember that just because everyone else is doing it, and the possible rewards are great, it doesn't mean you should too. Speculation's problem is the absence of real value in the investment, that is selling for a higher price than its real value. Sooner or later, gravity and reality will kick in without warning...

Conclusion

In conclusion, creating value and investing will increase your wealth over time, while also helping others grow and improve their lives as well.

I still prefer realestate to other kinds of investments. Maybe because I'm an architect, and my greatgrandfather, my grandfather and my father were also builders. I find great passion and rewards in rebuilding and adding value to abandoned buildings that no one likes, and realestate is, until we live in Mars and other planets, a very scarce and limited product, thus rising in value over time. You also get to keep it in case of an economic crisis, which in case of some companies and stocks might not happen, for the stockmarket is in its essence unpredictable, we only know for certain that sometimes it will go up and sometimes it will go down.

Never invest money you might need for your life or an emergency, and always keep a considerable ammount of cash in your bank in a savings account. That will allow you to buy great opportunities whenever they present themselves. That's why they say money creates money.

Remember, past growth and demand aren´t indicators of future growth and demand, so always do your own numbers and seek professional advice.

I have sometimes invested 100% of my capital in realestate, onetime even 120% being the 20% a small credit, but in the stock market and securities I have only invested 5%.

I choose to stay that way until the next great realestate opportunity comes along.

So, good luck with all your investments, I wish you a healthy, happy and prosperous life, and I hope to be hearing from you one day, talking about how well you did or about an investment you would like to make.

Godspeed,

Miguel Oliveira

i@bricoarts.com

Credits

www.bricoarts.com
© 2021 ®